# X-TREME FACTS: CONTINENTS

# SOUTH AMERICA

by Marcia Abramson

Minneapolis, Minnesota

**Credits:**
Title Page, vitmark/Shutterstock; 4 top left, Tupungato/Shutterstock; 4, Klaus Ulrich Mueller/Shutterstock; 4 bottom left, Vaclav Hroch/Shutterstock; 4 bottom right, 21 bottom left, Roman Samborskyi/Shutterstock; 5 top, hakanyalicn/Shutterstock.com; 5 top right, Brocreative/Shutterstock; 5 middle, Delpixel/Shutterstock; 5 bottom, Sobrevolando Patagonia/Shutterstock; 5 bottom left, 14 bottom middle, 8 bottom middle, 24 bottom left, Jeka/Shutterstock; 5 bottom right, sunsinger/Shutterstock.com; 6 top, G.Hüdepohl/ESO/Creative Commons; 6 bottom, ESO/S. Brunier/Creative Commons; 6 bottom left, Louella938/Shutterstock; 6 bottom right, Design Projects/Shutterstock; 7 top, Meyriane de Mira Teixeira/Creative Commons; 7 top left, Mihail Pustovit/Shutterstock; 7 top middle, Dejan Dundjerski/Shutterstock; 7 top right, Sabine Schoenfeld/Shutterstock; 7 middle, Alfredo Cerra/Shutterstock.com; 7 bottom, Pav-Pro Photography Ltd/Shutterstock; 7 bottom left, Lucy.Brown/Shutterstock.com; t7 bottom right, Krakenimages.com/Shutterstock; 8 top, Neil Palmer/CIAT/Creative Commons; 8 bottom, Jason Hollinger/Creative Commons; 8 bottom left, ja-aljona/Shutterstock.com; 8 bottom right, Kuznetcov_Konstantin/Shutterstock; 9 top, EEJCC/Creative Commons; 9 top left, 10 bottom left, LightField Studios/Shutterstock; 8 top right, Ekaterina McClaud/Shutterstock.com; 9 middle, Tyraelux/Creative Commons; 9 bottom, K_Boonnitrod/Shutterstock; 9 bottom right, Seumas Christie-Johnston/Shutterstock; 10, BW Press/Shutterstock.com; 10 bottom right, Paulo Jr/Shutterstock.com; 11 top, buladeviagensn/Shutterstock; 11 top left, A.P.S.Photography/Shutterstock.com; 11 top right, COULANGESn/Shutterstock; 11 middle, Dirk Erckenn/Shutterstock; 11 bottom, Ryan M. Boltonn/Shutterstock; 11 bottom right, RussieseOn/Shutterstock; 12, ixpert/Shutterstock; 12 left, Ekaterina Pokrovsky/Shutterstock; 12 right, saiko3p/Shutterstock; 13 top, kavram/Shutterstock; 13 top middle, IdKa/Shutterstock; 13 top right, Samuel Ericksen/Shutterstock; 13 middle, 13 bottom, R.M. Nunes/Shutterstock; 13 bottom left, 13 bottom right, Gorodenkoff/Shutterstock; 14 top, PsamatheM/Creative Commons; 14 bottom, Vadim Petrakov/Shutterstock; 15 top, sdecoret/Shutterstock; 15 top left, 15 top right, Design Projects/Shutterstock; 15 top middle, Diego Delso, delso.photo, License CC-BY-SA; 15 middle left, OSTILL is Franck Camhi/Shutterstock; 15 middle right, Sebastian Velasquez Mesa/Shutterstock; 15 bottom, Gavin Rough/cc-by-2.0; 15 bottom right, Sheila Fitzgerald/Shutterstock; 16 top, Bernard DUPONT/Creative Commons; 16 bottom, Toniflap/Shutterstock; 17 top right, Gerry Zambonini/Creative Commons; 17 top, Wirestock Creators/Shutterstock; 17 top middle, SL-Photography/Shutterstock.com; 17 middle, BearFotos/Shutterstock; 17 bottom, Thell Pereira/Creative Commons;18 top, Wildnerdpix/Shutterstock; 18 top middle, NH353/Creative Commons; 18 bottom, Julius Jääskeläinen/Creative Commons; 19 top, Hans Stieglitz/Creative Commons; 19 middle, MasterfulNerd/Creative Commons; 19 bottom, Maridav/Shutterstock; 19 bottom right, Structured Vision/Shutterstock; 20 top, Mayela Ore/Creative Commons; 20 bottom, Sofia Barchuk Alvarez/Creative Commons; 20 bottom left, Elena Berd/Shutterstock.com; 20 bottom middle, Daderot/Public Domain; 20 bottom right, Pierre André Leclercq/License CC-BY-SA;21 top, Ripio/Shutterstock; 21 top left, Pierre André/Creative Commons; 21 top right, 25 bottom right, Milton Rodriguez/Shutterstock.com; 21 middle left, Sailko/Creative Commons; 21 middle right, Rowanwindwhistler/Creative Commons; 21 bottom, Romerito Pontes/Creative Commons; 22 top, Ministerio de Defensa del Perú/Creative Commons; 22 bottom, Palácio do Planalto/Creative Commons; 22 bottom right, joi54/Shutterstock; 23 top, Dan Lundberg/Creative Commons; 23 top left, Sun_Shine/Shutterstock.com; 23 top middle, Yurii_Yarema/Shutterstock; 23 middle, Remi Jouan/GNU Free Documentation License; 23 bottom, Bjørn Christian Tørrissen/Creative Commons; 23 bottom left, Kabardins photo/Shutterstock; 24 top, Olga Bondas/Shutterstock; 24 bottom, flanovais/Shutterstock; 24 bottom right, William Moss/Shutterstock; 25 top, SALMONNEGRO-STOCK/Shutterstock; 25 top left, BearFotos/Shutterstock; 25 middle left, Leonel Delgado Gavidia/Shutterstock; 25 middle right, Gabriela Bertolini/Shutterstock; 25 bottom, Shanti Hesse/Shutterstock; 25 bottom left, Kilobug/Creative Commons; 26 top, Tutti Frutti/Shutterstock; 26 bottom, castromaca/Shutterstock.com; 26 bottom right, Bernardo Emanuelle/Shutterstock; 27 top, BlackBird07/Creative Commons; 27 top middle, Arturo Lopez Llontop/Shutterstock; 27 middle, Mark Green/Shutterstock.com; 27 bottom, A.RICARDO/Shutterstock; 28 top left, Damsea/Shutterstock; 28 bottom left, Sharp/Shutterstock; 28 top middle, Kozak Sergii/Shutterstock; 28 top right, Alexandr Makarov/Shutterstock; 28-29, Austen Photography

**Bearport Publishing Company Product Development Team**
President: Jen Jenson; Director of Product Development: Spencer Brinker; Managing Editor: Allison Juda; Associate Editor: Naomi Reich; Associate Editor: Tiana Tran; Art Director: Colin O'Dea; Designer: Elena Klinkner; Designer: Kayla Eggert; Product Development Assistant: Owen Hamlin

Produced for Bearport Publishing by BlueAppleWorks Inc.
Managing Editor: Melissa McClellan; Art Director: T.J. Choleva; Photo Research: Jane Reid

STATEMENT ON USAGE OF GENERATIVE ARTIFICIAL INTELLIGENCE
Bearport Publishing remains committed to publishing high-quality nonfiction books. Therefore, we restrict the use of generative AI to ensure accuracy of all text and visual components pertaining to a book's subject. See BearportPublishing.com for details.

*Library of Congress Cataloging-in-Publication Data*

Names: Abramson, Marcia, 1949- author.
Title: South America / by Marcia Abramson.
Description: Minneapolis, Minnesota : Bearport Publishing Company, 2024. | Series: X-treme facts: Continents | Includes bibliographical references and index.
Identifiers: LCCN 2023031459 (print) | LCCN 2023031460 (ebook) | ISBN 9798889164326 (library binding) | ISBN 9798889164401 (paperback) | ISBN 9798889164470 (ebook)
Subjects: LCSH: South America--Geography--Juvenile literature.
Classification: LCC F2208.5 A273 2024  (print) | LCC F2208.5  (ebook) | DDC 918--dc23/eng/20230718
LC record available at https://lccn.loc.gov/2023031459
LC ebook record available at https://lccn.loc.gov/2023031460

Copyright © 2024 Bearport Publishing Company. All rights reserved. No part of this publication may be reproduced in whole or in part, stored in any retrieval system, or transmitted in any form or by any means, electronic, mechanical, photocopying, recording, or otherwise, without written permission from the publisher.

For more information, write to Bearport Publishing, 5357 Penn Avenue South, Minneapolis, MN 55419.

# Contents

**A Continent of Contrasts** 4
**Climate Extremes** 6
**So Much Water** 8
**The Largest Rain Forest** 10
**Heading South** 12
**Spectacular Sights** 14
**Awesome Animals of South America** 16
**Evolutionary Islands** 18
**The Many People of South America** 20
**Vibrant Cities** 22
**Fabulous Food** 24
**Extreme Fun** 26

Make a Sloth 28
Glossary 30
Read More 31
Learn More Online 31
Index 32
About the Author 32

# A Continent of Contrasts

Where is the world's driest desert and the wettest rain forest? They're both in South America! Contrast is the name of the game across the continent's 7 million square miles (18 million sq km). Most of the land is covered in **tropical** forests. But there are also dry deserts, flat grasslands, tall mountains, and even frozen **glaciers**. Although most people live in cities, some make their homes across the countryside. Let's explore this extreme continent!

South America is the fourth-largest continent.

**Brazil takes up half of South America,** and about half of the continent's people live there, too.

WHY IS THIS BEACH SO CROWDED?

WELL, YOU AND THE REST OF BRAZIL HAD THE SAME IDEA.

South America is home to about 440 million people.

Most South Americans speak Spanish or Portuguese, but more than 500 **Indigenous** languages are also spoken across the continent.

**The Andes are the tallest mountains in South America.** They run along the entire west side of the continent.

Cowboys called gauchos ride horses through the grasslands of South America.

# Climate Extremes

It's hot and humid all year long in most of South America, especially in the Amazon River **basin**. But you can escape the heat by taking a trip to the beaches along the Atlantic Ocean or by trekking high up into the snowy Andes Mountains. If you can't decide between hot and cold, Chile and Argentina have both! Desert heat scorches the northern parts of these countries, but you'll need a jacket to face the freeze in the south.

The Atacama Desert in Argentina and Peru gets less than 0.2 inches (5 mm) of rain a year—**the least precipitation of any place on Earth.**

Scientists believe the harsh conditions in the Atacama Desert may be similar to those on the surface of Mars!

**Chocó, Colombia, has the wettest rain forest in the world.** It rains more than 300 days a year.

Chocó gets more than 33 feet (10 m) of rain each year.

**Blizzards often blow through the Andes.** In July 2022, more than 400 people were trapped by a storm's heavy snow.

**Argentina holds the record** for both the hottest and coldest temperatures in South America.

The country has reached a high of 120 degrees Fahrenheit (49 degrees Celsius) and a low of -27°F (-33°C).

# So Much Water

The Amazon River is the longest and most famous river in South America. But it isn't the only one. The Orinoco and the Paraná are two other huge rivers. People have traveled in boats on these flowing waterways for thousands of years. Today, the rivers' many waterfalls are used to make electric power. But there's even more wonderful water. There are hundreds of freshwater lakes in the Andes Mountains, and the entire continent sits between the Atlantic and Pacific Oceans.

The Amazon River flows for nearly 4,000 miles (6,400 km).

In 2011, scientists discovered slow-moving water **deep underground below the Amazon.**

WHERE ARE YOU GOING? THEY SAID THE WATER WAS UNDERGROUND.

DON'T WORRY, I HAVE A SHOVEL!

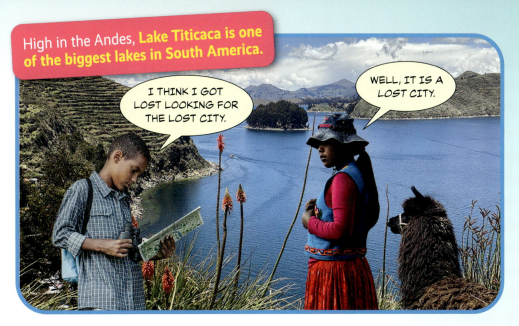

There are stories of a lost city hidden at the bottom of Lake Titicaca. In 2000, divers found the **ruins** of an ancient temple deep below the surface.

Iguazu Falls on the border of Argentina and Brazil are both taller and wider than Niagara Falls.

# The Largest Rain Forest

South America's longest river flows through a huge rain forest of the same name—the Amazon! This lush forest gets about 12 ft (4 m) of rain every year. But the Amazon is so full of plants it can take as long as 10 minutes for rain to make its way from the top leaves in the **canopy** down to the forest floor. More **species** of plants and animals live in the Amazon Rain Forest than anywhere else in the world.

The Amazon is the world's largest rain forest.

The Amazon Rain Forest covers about 2 million square miles (6 million sq km) and has almost 400 billion trees.

More than 400 communities call the Amazon home. **Many of these groups rely on the forest for food and water.**

IS IT HARD TO GET SUPPLIES AROUND HERE?

NO, IT'S EASY! WE GET ALL OUR STUFF FROM AMAZON.

DO YOU KNOW WHERE THIS RIVER GOES?

I'M NOT SURE. I'M KIND OF NEW AROUND HERE.

In 2014 and 2015 alone, scientists discovered 381 new kinds of plants and animals in the rain forest, including a new species of pink river dolphin!

**Beware!** Piranhas, poison frogs, and other dangerous critters live in the Amazon.

More than 2.5 million different species of insects live in this rain forest.

The rain forest is where you'll find the Amazonian giant centipede. These creepy crawlies are **venomous**, and can grow to 12 in. (30 cm) long!

11

# Heading South

Though quite different, Patagonia is also pretty amazing. This region covering the southern tip of South America has the Andes Mountains in the west and dry deserts and grasslands in the east. Patagonia spans about 260,000 square miles (670,000 sq km), but there are only about 2 million people living there. Still, visitors to the area aren't disappointed by this region's spectacular nature and landscapes.

There are more penguins in Patagonia than people.

PATAGONIA IS GETTING CROWDED. MAYBE I SHOULD MOVE TO ANTARCTICA.

Ushuaia in Argentina is the southernmost city in the world.

The tip of South America is only about 620 miles (1,000 km) away from Antarctica.

Mountains in Patagonia are home to the largest of the world's remaining herds of wild horses.

Scientists believe the drawings in the Cave of the Hands in the Patagonian Desert could be about 13,000 years old.

# Spectacular Sights

The jaw-dropping views in South America aren't only in Patagonia. To see another one, climb Aconcagua Mountain—the tallest peak in the Andes, reaching almost 23,000 ft (7,000 m) into the sky. At a lower elevation, Laguna Colorada in Bolivia is a shallow salt lake that looks bright red. The lake's color comes from the red **algae** living in the water. There are extreme natural wonders and a lot of incredible history to see all over South America.

**The world's largest salt flat can be found in Bolivia.** When nearby lakes overflow, the water turns the land into a stunning natural mirror.

I LOOK PRETTY GOOD IN LAKE WATER!

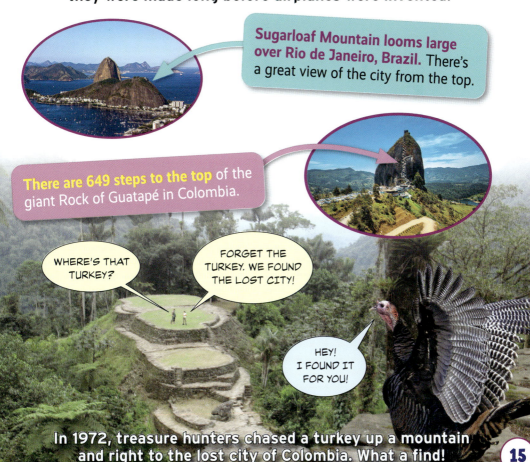

# Awesome Animals of South America

With so many climates and **habitats**, it's no wonder there are all kinds of animals in South America. In fact, Brazil has the greatest variety of plant and animal species of any country in the world. It has more than 1,800 species of birds alone! Some animals, such as wild guinea pigs and black caimans, are found only in South America. Let's go on a wildlife adventure!

**The jaguar is the largest wild cat in the Americas.**

Jaguars have spots that help them blend in with their jungle homes.

Black caimans are top **predators** of the Amazon. **They can grow up to 15 ft (5 m) long.**

Toucans' beaks can be almost half as long as their bodies.

YOU WOULDN'T SPIT ON ME, WOULD YOU?

NOT AS LONG AS YOU KEEP GIVING ME SNACKS.

Furry llamas and alpacas are the South American cousins of camels. They are known for their soft wool and tendency to spit when bothered.

**Andean condors are the world's largest birds of prey.** Their wings can span up to 11 ft (3 m) across.

**Capybaras are the world's largest rodents.** They are excellent swimmers, spending a lot of time in the waters throughout South America.

WHY ARE YOU SO DIRTY?

I WAS GETTING A LITTLE HOT.

Capybaras roll in mud to stay cool.

# Evolutionary Islands

The Galápagos Islands are just 600 miles (1,000 km) off the coast of mainland South America. Millions of years ago, animals flew, drifted, or swam from the continent to these **uninhabited** islands. While separated from other animals of their kind, the creatures **evolved** as they adapted to survive in their new home. Many have become some of the most **unique** animals in all of South America—and the world!

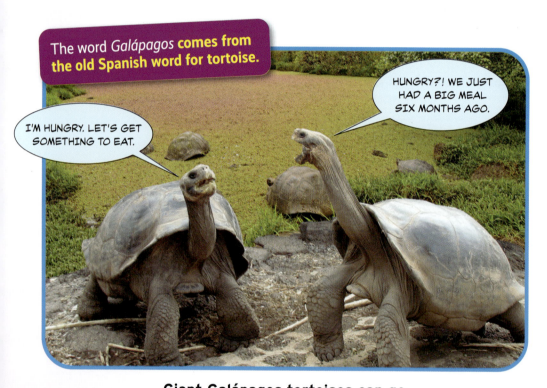

The word *Galápagos* comes from the old Spanish word for tortoise.

I'M HUNGRY. LET'S GET SOMETHING TO EAT.

HUNGRY?! WE JUST HAD A BIG MEAL SIX MONTHS AGO.

Giant Galápagos tortoises can go without food or water for an entire year!

A trip to the Galápagos helped scientist Charles Darwin come up with the **theory** of evolution in 1835.

Boobies with deeper blue feet have better luck finding a mate than those with pale blue feet.

The only seagoing lizards on the planet are the marine iguanas of the Galápagos Islands.

# The Many People of South America

People first arrived in South America about 14,000 years ago. Since then, the continent has been home to many great **civilizations**. In the 1400s, the Inca Empire spread across what is modern-day Ecuador, Peru, Bolivia, Argentina, and Chile. Inca peoples built roads and carved steps in the mountainsides for farms. They crafted with gold and made beautiful fabrics. Let's learn more about some of the many incredible civilizations of South America.

Norte Chico in Peru was the first civilization in the Americas. It existed about 5,000 years ago.

I THINK YOUR NUMBERS ARE OFF. CAN I READ YOUR RECORDS?

SURE, MY QUIPU IS RIGHT THERE.

The Incas did not have a system of writing. They kept records using special knotted strings called quipus.

Today, nearly half of Peru's people are **descended** from the Incas and speak the Incan language of Quechua.

The Nazca civilization in what is now Peru was known for its unique **pottery**. The people there made bowls and jars, sometimes in the shape of human heads.

The Guaraní people built large homes that provided shelter for extended family groups.

# Vibrant Cities

South America's big, modern cities are also pretty spectacular. That's probably part of the reason why almost 80 percent of South Americans live in a city. Street musicians play tunes and vendors sell tasty snacks late into the night. During the day, cities are full of people visiting local markets and museums. From Buenos Aires to Lima, there's a lot of South American urban life to explore.

Cities have been on the site known today as Lima, Peru, since about 200 BCE!

About 22 million people live in São Paulo, Brazil. It's the world's fourth-largest city!

I CAN SEE OUR HOTEL FROM HERE. WE'LL BE THERE IN NO TIME.

WE MIGHT GET STUCK IN SOME SERIOUS AIR TRAFFIC!

São Paulo also has the largest number of helicopters and the most helicopter traffic in the world.

Be sure to catch the Witches' Market of La Paz, Bolivia. There, you can buy anything from spices and candles to animal bones and spells.

Museo del Oro in Bogotá, Colombia, **is home to one of the world's largest collections of ancient gold treasures.**

# Fabulous Food

Luckily, delicious food can be found in both the cities and the countrysides of South America. All over the continent, people turn local crops and seafood into amazing dishes. Peruvians make a dish called ceviche from raw fish and lemon or lime juice. In Argentina, hand-sized pies called empanadas are filled with beef, cheese, vegetables, or fruits. And almost everyone in South America eats fried plantains, a banana-like fruit. If you come to visit, be sure to come hungry!

**Potatoes have been growing in the Andes Mountains for thousands of years.** Andean potatoes can be red, pink, yellow, blue, or bright purple!

The national dish of Brazil is feijoada. It's a stew made of pork and beans.

WHERE CAN I GET SOME FEIJOADA?

IT'S OUR NATIONAL DISH. YOU CAN PROBABLY FIND IT ANYWHERE!

Brazil is nicknamed the coffee pot of the world because it grows the most coffee beans. However, Colombian coffee is often considered the best in South America.

In Argentina, a dessert called pastelitos is eaten to celebrate Independence Day. **The flaky pastry is deep fried and filled with sweet potato paste.**

In Venezuela, fluffy corn pancakes called arepas are **a tasty Christmas treat.**

Quinoa is an ancient grain from the Andes. Today, it's become popular as a healthy superfood.

# Extreme Fun

Want to celebrate? South America is the place to go! Catch a soccer match for some serious fun. When their favorite teams are playing, many South Americans get together to watch the excitement. And soccer is not the only reason to get together. There are festivals and celebrations, both small and large, every day in South America. What's not to celebrate when you live on such an amazing, extreme continent?

**The tango got its start in Argentina.** By 1915, the dance was a worldwide craze!

Argentina and Brazil **are huge soccer rivals.**

WE WON THE CUP!

BIG DEAL! WE'VE STILL WON MORE CUPS THAN YOU!

Argentinians brag about winning the 2022 World Cup. However, Brazil has five world titles while Argentina has only three.

Peru's biggest soccer stadium has 80,093 seats. It could hold every person who lives in Gary, Indiana.

**Peru celebrates Inti Raymi,** the colorful Inca sun festival, on June 24.

**Rio de Janeiro's Carnival is the world's biggest party.** Millions of people crowd the streets for parades full of colorful costumes.

# Make a Sloth

## Craft Project

The sloths of South America's rain forests are the world's slowest mammal. They take things easy to help **conserve** their energy. So, they spend most of their time hanging upside down from trees. Make your own cute sloth!

Sloths don't drink very often! They get most of their water by chewing on leaves, twigs, and fruit.

### What You Will Need

- Scissors
- A piece of dark-brown construction paper
- A piece of light-brown construction paper
- A black marker
- Glue
- A pencil

CAN I GET A LITTLE PRIVACY, PLEASE?

Sloths climb down from their tree homes once a week to go to the bathroom.

## Step One

Cut out the shape of a sloth from the dark-brown piece of construction paper and set aside.

## Step Two

Cut an oval from the light-brown construction paper. This will be the face. Draw eyes, a nose, and a mouth on the oval with a black maker.

## Step Three

Glue the small oval face to the sloth body. Use a marker to draw claws on the feet.

## Step Four

Put some glue on the back of the arms. Wrap the arms, glue-side down, around the pencil. Hold it tightly for a couple of minutes to make sure your sloth sticks.

**algae** tiny plantlike living things that live and grow in water

**basin** the area that a river system covers

**canopy** the top layer of leaves and branches covering a forest

**civilizations** large groups of people that share the same history and ways of life

**conserve** to stop something from being wasted

**descended** came from humans who lived in an earlier time

**evolved** changed slowly and naturally over time

**glaciers** huge pieces of thick ice and snow

**habitats** places in nature where plants and animals normally live

**Indigenous** the people that originally lived and may continue to live in a place

**pottery** objects, such as bowls and plates, that are made of baked clay

**predators** animals that hunt and eat other animals

**ruins** parts of buildings or structures that are still left after a long time has passed

**species** groups that animals are divided into, according to similar characteristics

**theory** an idea or belief based on limited information

**tropical** having to do with the warm areas near the middle of Earth

**uninhabited** having no people living there

**unique** one of a kind, unlike any other

**venomous** able to inject poison by a sting or a bite

# Read More

**Kerry, Isaac.** *Spotlight on Brazil (Countries on the World Stage).* Minneapolis: Lerner Publications, 2024.

**Levsey, Dylan.** *South America.* Huntington Beach, CA: Teacher Created Materials, Inc, 2023.

**Vonder Brink, Tracy.** *South America (Seven Continents of the World).* New York: Crabtree Publishing Company, 2023.

# Learn More Online

1. Go to **www.factsurfer.com** or scan the QR code below.

2. Enter **"X-treme South America"** into the search box.

3. Click on the cover of this book to see a list of websites.

# Index

Amazon Rain Forest  10–12

Amazon River  6, 8, 10

Andes Mountains  5–9, 12, 14, 21, 24–25

Angel Falls  9

animals  10–11, 16, 18

Argentina  6–7, 9, 20, 24–26

Atacama Desert  6

Bolivia  14, 20, 23

Brazil  4, 9, 15–16, 22, 24–26

Chile  6, 13, 20, 23

Chocó, Colombia  7

Ecuador  20

Galápagos Islands  18–19

Iguazu Falls  9

Incas  20–21, 27

insects  11

Lake Titicaca  9

languages  5, 21

Machu Picchu  21

Patagonia  12–13

Peru  6, 15, 20–22, 24, 27

sloth  28–29

Venezuela  9, 25

# About the Author

Marcia Abramson lives and went to school in Ann Arbor, Michigan, where she learned about South American language and culture.